101
Ways to
Read
With
Speed
and
Understanding

101 Ways to Read With Speed and Understanding

by Denise Bieniek

illustrated by Barbara Levy

Troll

Printed in the United States of America.

10 9 8 7 6 5 4

To my mom,
who instilled in me a love of books.

CONTENTS

Chapter 1

Reading— A Gateway to the Past, Present, and Future

You look in your assignment pad and see the following list of things to do:

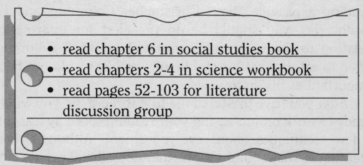

- read chapter 6 in social studies book
- read chapters 2-4 in science workbook
- read pages 52-103 for literature discussion group

Instead of wishing for less homework (which never works) try learning how to become a more efficient reader. The more efficient you become, the faster your reading will be, and the more time you will have for other things.

How can you become a more efficient reader? The first step is to realize that different reading material requires a different rate of speed. For example, if you are reading a novel, you will most likely read faster than if you are reading a chapter in a science textbook. The material in your textbook requires greater concentration, so you will probably read more slowly to absorb as much information as possible.

The second step is to learn *decoding* skills (to decode is to figure out what a word means). There are many different methods of decoding, and the more ways you know, the better decoder you will be. This book will explain some of the most useful decoding methods.

In addition to decoding, you will need to learn how to read for understanding. Simply knowing the meaning of the words you read is not enough; you must also know what these words mean when they are put together to form thoughts. You must know how to sort out which part of the text is important and which is not. For example, if you are reading a passage about Christopher Columbus and his discoveries, you should be on the alert for information relating to the topic. Information about what Columbus liked to eat or what his childhood was like would not be as important as his discoveries.

After you have mastered the first three steps, you will be ready to work on increasing your reading speed by learning a few techniques about eye movement. Although these techniques may sound simple, they actually take quite a bit of practice and concentration before you can master them. Anyone can read faster by skimming through the text. That is not the purpose of this book. Instead, you must learn comprehension, combined with speed. After all, what good would it do to read faster if you have no idea what you just read?

Remember, the secret to being a *faster* reader is to be an *efficient* reader. Know what *type of material* you are reading, and set your pace accordingly. Use *decoding* skills on any words you do not know. Decide what is *important* to the topic and what is not. And above all—*understand* what you are reading!

Chapter 2

What Kind of Reader Are You?

1. Start a reading journal. This is a great place to make lists of the books you've read, jot down unfamiliar word definitions, and note concepts you don't understand. You can also practice drills for increasing your reading comprehension and speed in your journal.

2. Try to determine what kind of reader you are. There are three basic types:

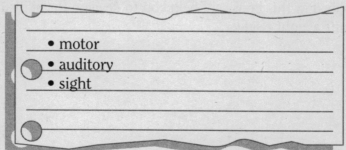

- motor
- auditory
- sight

3. A **motor reader** moves some part of his or her body while reading. Do you wiggle your foot or tap your fingers while you read? Do you have to move your finger along a line as you read in order to understand the concept being discussed? Then you are a motor reader. If the movement stops, most likely your comprehension decreases; this is because your reading habit has been disturbed.

4. An **auditory reader** needs to hear the words as he or she reads. This group is quite varied, and ranges from people who need to say the words aloud as they read to those who "speak" the words inside their heads as they read. Auditory readers like to read either with external noise or absolutely no noise at all. Any disruption in their ideal conditions decreases their comprehension level.

5. A **sight reader** can understand what he or she is reading right away. There is no dependence on moving a part of the body or hearing the words as they are read. Sight reading is the fastest way to read, and the techniques described in this book will help you to develop the skills to become a sight reader.

6. There are different levels of comprehension. The purpose of the reading you do will determine the level of comprehension you will need. The different levels are:

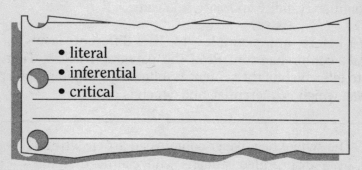

- literal
- inferential
- critical

7. Literal comprehension means you can restate the ideas and information from your reading in your own words. You understand the words and the grammar used, you can recall the main idea, and you know the sequence of information presented.

8. Inferential comprehension means you can explain ideas and information from your reading that were not explicitly stated. You understand the author's purpose and attitude, and you infer facts, main ideas, comparisons, and cause-and-effect relationships not directly stated. Your past experiences and background are used as a basis for your hypotheses, and you are able to add your own thoughts to what the author was trying to say.

9. Critical comprehension means you can analyze and evaluate the ideas and information found in your reading. You can make judgments of reality vs. fantasy, fact vs. opinion, validity, morality, and value.

10. Here are examples of the different levels of comprehension. Read the paragraph below. Then try to tell which of the sentences following the paragraph is literal, which is inferential, and which is critical.

The school newspaper contains an article written by a disgruntled student who claims that the cafeteria food is not fit for human consumption. The author retells an experience that occurred the other day when she saw some less-than-fresh fruit being served as dessert. The author includes a survey of the entire fifth and sixth grades, and concludes from it that a new food service should be used.

a. Tom goes home and tells his parents about the article, reciting several facts from it.

b. Brian tells his friends that they should organize and picket the lunch room based upon what he read in the article.

c. Cissy feels that the author wanted to get students' attention because she is running for class president.

---

11. You have a built-in comprehension radar—your memory! Your own experiences and background have enormous impact on your comprehension skills. For example, say you are reading about sailing and you live in a place with no oceans or lakes nearby. You would probably have little knowledge of sailing; therefore, your understanding of the subject might be quite low.

The opposite is also true. If you are assigned to read about life on a farm and you live on a farm, your comprehension of the subject would be quite high because you would have experienced many of the things discussed in the reading. Use your own experiences every time you read. They are important.

12. When you're reading, be sure to focus. If there are too many distractions, your comprehension level will plummet. If possible, try to find an out-of-the-way place to do your reading. Or make a "Do Not Disturb" sign to put on your door to minimize interruptions.

13. Adjust your speed of reading to the material you are reading. For example, your rate of speed will be faster if you are reading a novel for fun, reading something you are interested in, or if you are skimming a block of text for a specific item. Your rate will probably be slower if you are reading technical material, stuff you are not really interested in, or if you are studying for a test.

14. If you cannot understand something or if you want to make sure you thoroughly understand a particular concept, slow your reading speed. If you are familiar with the material you are reading, go a little faster.

15. If the material you are reading is tough to understand, reread it and try to restate it in your own words. If it is still too hard, read just a few pages at a time. Restate the main concepts you've just read and then go on to the next few pages. You may also find it helpful to jot down key points on index cards. You can write a question on one side and the answer on the other. Go back to the cards after you've finished reading the material and quiz yourself. Once you are sure you understand the main ideas, move on to the next section.

16. For especially complex reading material, divide the reading into paragraphs. After each paragraph, try to restate the information you've just read in your own words. When you can do this successfully go on to the next paragraph. Take a break, then go back and reread the material at a faster pace, making sure you understand all the important concepts.

17. Follow these hints to help you when you come upon a word you do not know:

- Read on and go back to the word when you finish the paragraph. Does it make sense now?
- Look the word up in a dictionary.
- Use your phonics skills to sound out the word.
- Is there a prefix? What is the root word? Is there a suffix? Divide the word up into parts and try to figure out its meaning.

If you stop in the middle of your reading to try to figure out what a word means or how it is pronounced, you will lose the sense of what you are reading. Keep going and return to the word later if necessary. Underline or highlight the word so you can find it quickly.

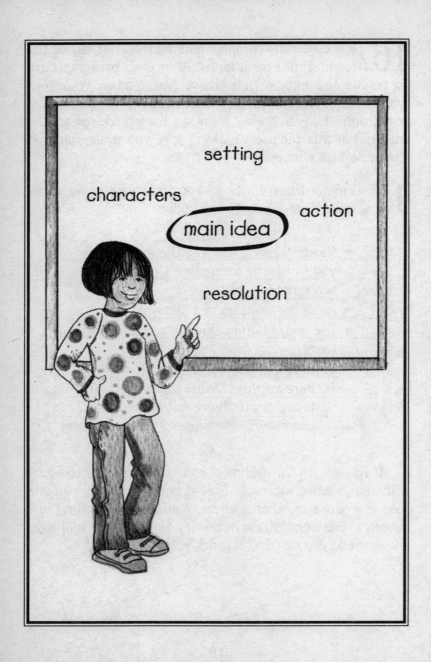

Chapter 3

How You Read Depends on What You Read

18. There are two basic types of writing: **narrative** and **expository**. Narrative writing presents true or fictional stories and is usually found in literature. The writing style is fluid and easygoing, similar to our speech patterns in friendly conversation. Expository writing provides information and facts, and is what you usually find in textbooks. This writing style is sometimes more formal. Often there are many facts and complex concepts presented in a few sentences. Narrative and expository writing both give us ideas and information, but they present the material in different ways. Therefore, you must use different reading strategies for each type.

19. Here are some tips for improving your comprehension skills when reading a narrative.

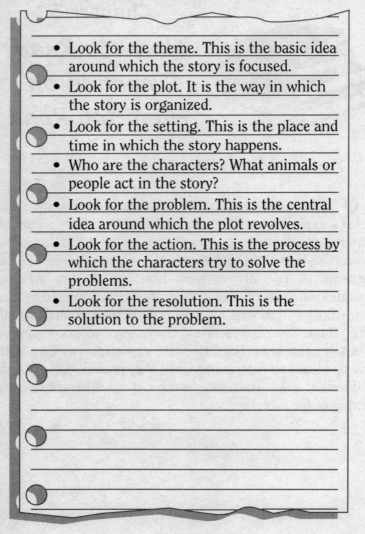

- Look for the theme. This is the basic idea around which the story is focused.
- Look for the plot. It is the way in which the story is organized.
- Look for the setting. This is the place and time in which the story happens.
- Who are the characters? What animals or people act in the story?
- Look for the problem. This is the central idea around which the plot revolves.
- Look for the action. This is the process by which the characters try to solve the problems.
- Look for the resolution. This is the solution to the problem.

20. There are different types of expository writing. If you know the different types, you will be better able to understand the material you are reading. Each one presents information in its own way.

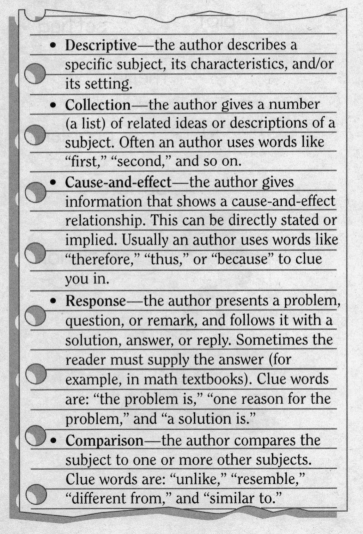

- **Descriptive**—the author describes a specific subject, its characteristics, and/or its setting.

- **Collection**—the author gives a number (a list) of related ideas or descriptions of a subject. Often an author uses words like "first," "second," and so on.

- **Cause-and-effect**—the author gives information that shows a cause-and-effect relationship. This can be directly stated or implied. Usually an author uses words like "therefore," "thus," or "because" to clue you in.

- **Response**—the author presents a problem, question, or remark, and follows it with a solution, answer, or reply. Sometimes the reader must supply the answer (for example, in math textbooks). Clue words are: "the problem is," "one reason for the problem," and "a solution is."

- **Comparison**—the author compares the subject to one or more other subjects. Clue words are: "unlike," "resemble," "different from," and "similar to."

See if you can identify which type of expository writing form is used in each of the following paragraphs.

Families come in all shapes and sizes. Years ago, when someone said "family," many people had an image of a mother, father, and children, with grandparents, aunts, and uncles living nearby. Today, families can have anywhere from two people on up. Some typical family groups are: father and child; grandmother, grandfather, and children; mother, grandmother, and children; husband and wife; stepfamilies; and mother, father, and adopted child. _____

To become a teacher, one must first get good grades. Colleges look for applicants who are successful in high school, as well as involved in activities outside of school. After completing your first four years, you must then study at graduate school. The next step is to apply to the Board of Education in the area in which you wish to teach. You must take the board's exams and be interviewed. If you qualify, a school will be found for you, or you may go out for interviews with the principals of the schools of your choice. You will be put on probation for a few years, and finally, be granted tenure if all goes well. _____

For many years, plant life flourished in our local area. With the rising popularity of the area, more and more families decided to move here. More people meant more housing, more schools, and more businesses. The roads became clogged with traffic during rush hours. Garbage disposal became a problem. As a result of all of this development, the woods have been cut down, the river is polluted, and the air quality on muggy days is unhealthy. _____

Public transportation is one problem the city must solve. Subway riders are constantly bombarded with announcements about trains being delayed, rerouted, and taken out of service. The stations are crowded, dirty, and in some cases, unsafe. The city claims there is no money for renovations. Several solutions have been proposed by citizen groups: hire a new transportation manager committed to redoing the subways; raise money by lobbying legislators; heighten the public's awareness and organize protests; boycott the subways; organize a citizen group to clean up each station. _____

The Grand Canyon is different from any other place in the United States. It is bigger than any other canyon. Its natural beauty is overwhelming. The number of tourists who visit the Grand Canyon has risen steadily over the years as its popularity has increased. _____

Chapter 4
Decoding: Tracking Down Clues to Word Identification

21. If you come across a word you do not know while you are reading, don't panic! Finish reading the paragraph, then paraphrase what you've just read. Now go back to the unfamiliar word. Can you figure out its meaning now? The rest of the paragraph may offer clues to help you understand the word.

22. Knowing letter sounds is one way to figure out words. Here's a quick review of short vowel sounds:

ă	add	quack	vast
ĕ	fresh	spell	zest
ĭ	dim	sister	whiskers
ŏ	forgot	pocket	smog
ŭ	crumb	muck	sprung

These are long vowel sounds:

$\bar{a}$	drape	lane	trade
$\bar{e}$	we	he	beet
$\bar{i}$	hive	slice	tribe
$\bar{o}$	chrome	quote	throne
$\bar{u}$	cube	mule	tune

digraphs

$\overline{ai}$ (long a)	daily	praise	raid
$\overline{ay}$ (long a)	hay	say	stray
$\overline{ea}$ (long e)	eagle	leap	teach
$\overline{ee}$ (long e)	beech	speech	wheel
$\overline{oa}$ (long o)	gloat	oak	toast
oo (boot)	booster	noose	snooze
oo (book)	cook	moor	soot
ue	clue	fuel	true

diphthongs

au	austere	saunter	laundry
aw	awesome	flaw	straw
ew	askew	review	threw
oi	appoint	foist	turmoil
ou	bough	found	impound
ow	bower	powder	yowl
oy	cloy	destroy	royal

23. A root word is a word that cannot be broken down into parts. If you have trouble figuring out a word, try to break it down to its root. Take away prefixes, suffixes, endings, or a compound partner and see if you know the word. Combine your knowledge of the root word with the meaning of the other parts and see what happens.

24. A prefix is a syllable, group of syllables, or word that is added to the beginning of a root word, and changes the root word's meaning to form a new word. Being able to recognize common prefixes will help you quickly learn new words if you already know the root word. Some common prefixes are:

Prefix	Meaning	Example
a-, ab-	away from	abnormal
anti-	against	antifreeze
auto-	self	autobiography
bi-	two	bicycle
co-	together, with	coexist
counter-	against	counterclockwise
dis-	apart from, not	discontinue
extra-	outside, beyond	extraordinary
fore-	in front	foreground
in-	not	inadmissible
inter-	between, among	intermix
mid-	middle	midday
mis-	wrong	misstep
non-	not	nonviolent
over-	over	overactive
pre-	before	predate
re-	again	relive
super-	over	superhighway
tele-	far away	telescope
un-	not	uneven

25. A suffix is a syllable, group of syllables, or word added to the end of a root word, and changes the root word's meaning to form a new word. Recognizing common suffixes will help you learn the meanings of new words if you know the root word. Some common suffixes are:

Suffix	Meaning	Example
-able	able to	enjoyable
-al	relating to	electrical
-ary, -ery	that which, place where	bakery
-er	one who, that which	grocer
-er	more	lighter
-est	most	latest
-ful	full of	skillful
-hood	state or rank	childhood
-ist	one who	artist
-ish	having nature of	foolish
-less	without	penniless
-ly	in the manner of	quietly
-ment	resulting action or state	payment
-ness	state of being	sickness
-ous	condition	nervous
-tion, -ion	act, process, state	election

26. A compound word is a word consisting of two or more root words. Knowing what the root words are will help you figure out the meaning of the compound word. What do you think the following compound words mean? If you are unsure of the definitions of these words, look them up in a dictionary. How many did you correctly identify?

ballpark	goldfish
bedroom	highway
bookend	junkyard
catnap	landmark
countryman	pancake
drugstore	townspeople
everybody	underside
flagship	vineyard
football	waterfall
footprint	windmill
freestyle	yourself

27. Nouns are words that name a person, place, or thing. In the English language, there are regular nouns and irregular nouns. To make a regular noun plural, just add an *s*. When you make an irregular noun plural, you sometimes have to change the ending or the middle. Some nouns just stay the same whether they are singular or plural. There is no hard and fast rule for all irregular nouns. The only way to know the plural forms is to memorize them.

Some nouns have no singular form. Don't be fooled by these nouns. If you are not sure, reread the word, the sentence it is in, and the paragraph it is in. One hint is to look at the verb in the sentence. Is it plural or singular?

Regular nouns made plural		Irregular nouns made plural		Nouns with no singular form
girl	girls	leaf	leaves	data
table	tables	child	children	suds
flower	flowers	mouse	mice	sheep
car	cars	man	men	deer
door	doors	tomato	tomatoes	
		baby	babies	
		moose	moose	

28. A verb tells us that an action is taking place. Verbs can be deceptive. When the action is taking place now, it is called **present tense**. When the action already took place, it is called **past tense**. Regular verbs usually add -*d,* or -*ed* to the end when they are in the past tense. Irregular verbs change, sometimes greatly, when they are put in the past tense.

Regular verbs in present and past tense		Irregular verbs in present and past tense	
walk	walked	run	ran
watch	watched	see	saw
discuss	discussed	am	was
paint	painted	drive	drove
smell	smelled	fly	flew
		think	thought

29. Take the time to learn to identify nouns and verbs within a sentence. You will improve your reading speed and comprehension quickly, because these words are usually the most important and informational words in the sentence.

30. Antonyms are pairs of nouns that mean the opposite of each other. Learn pairs of antonyms to increase your vocabulary and your reading comprehension! Here are some pairs of antonyms:

above—below	future—past
advance—retreat	hard—soft
ancient—modern	minor—major
bore—excite	native—foreign
bright—dim	prohibit—permit
compliment—criticize	falsehood—truth
disperse—gather	smile—frown
exceed—fail	vacant—full

31. Homonyms are words that sound the same but have different meanings. If you come across one of these words, you need to make sure you have the right meaning. Use the surrounding text to help you determine which meaning is right. Here are some pairs of homonyms:

air—heir	groan—grown
ate—eight	idle—idol—idyll
bow—bough	insight—incite
carat—carrot	medal—metal—mettle
except—accept	new—knew—gnu
fair—fare	raise—raze
forth—fourth	sight—site—cite
gorilla—guerrilla	wait—weight

32. Synonyms are words that have the same meaning. If you learn some synonyms for each new word you discover, you will be expanding your vocabulary. The more words you know, the faster you will read, because you won't have to stop and decode unfamiliar words.

33. Some words have more than one meaning. If you do not know which meaning to use when reading, look at the words and grammar in the sentences surrounding it. They should give you a clue as to which meaning is correct. If you are still unsure, look each word up in the dictionary.

34. Punctuation can provide you with clues to the meaning as well as the delivery of the reading material. Here are examples of how the meaning of this sentence is changed depending upon the punctuation used.

> Lara said the teacher is so interesting.
> "Lara," said the teacher, "is so interesting."
> Lara said, "The teacher is so interesting."

The first example lets us know someone else is talking about what Lara said. The second example lets us know that the teacher is talking to someone about Lara. The last example lets us know that Lara is talking to someone about the teacher.

Now here are some examples that change the tone of the material:

> The snow is falling harder than ever.
> The snow is falling harder than ever!
> The snow is falling harder than ever?

The first sentence tells us the snow is falling harder than ever—it is a **declarative** statement and ends with a period. The second sentence tells us this fact is exciting, or frightening, or somewhat more urgent than the first—it is an **exclamatory** statement and ends with an exclamation point. The last statement is an **interrogative** one—it asks a question and ends with a question mark. An **imperative** statement tells someone to do something and can end with a period or an exclamation point.

35. Another trick for decoding words and their meanings is to divide multisyllabic words into monosyllables. That is, try to break an unknown word into its smaller parts, or syllables, if possible. By reading a word in smaller chunks, you might have a better chance of sounding it out and figuring out its meaning.

Remember these general rules for syllabication:

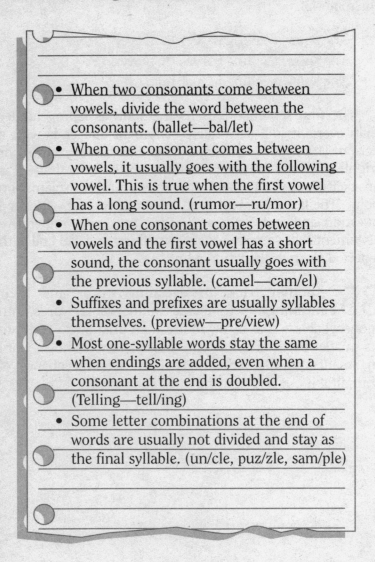

- When two consonants come between vowels, divide the word between the consonants. (ballet—bal/let)
- When one consonant comes between vowels, it usually goes with the following vowel. This is true when the first vowel has a long sound. (rumor—ru/mor)
- When one consonant comes between vowels and the first vowel has a short sound, the consonant usually goes with the previous syllable. (camel—cam/el)
- Suffixes and prefixes are usually syllables themselves. (preview—pre/view)
- Most one-syllable words stay the same when endings are added, even when a consonant at the end is doubled. (Telling—tell/ing)
- Some letter combinations at the end of words are usually not divided and stay as the final syllable. (un/cle, puz/zle, sam/ple)

36. Try to figure out the meanings of the following words. If you have trouble break the words into syllables and try again.

articulation	notoriety
caricature	paraphrase

Were you able to decipher the meaning of these words? Check below to see if you were right.

articulation—the act of putting a thought into words.

caricature—a distortion of a person, place, or event.

notoriety—the state of being notorious, or well known.

paraphrase—to restate something in one's own words.

37. Invest in a good dictionary and use it. A dictionary gives you the pronunciation of words, their parts of speech, meanings, spellings, and new words derived from the originals.

Each day, look up a few new words and try to memorize them. Your reading comprehension will increase as you build your vocabulary.

38. A thesaurus is a useful book as well. A basic thesaurus gives you the correct spellings of words, their parts of speech, and a choice of synonyms. When you read, you may notice that an author uses several different words to describe the same thing. That author probably used a thesaurus.

39. Similes describe a person, place, thing, feeling, idea, or action by comparing it to something else. Here are some examples of similes:

> My fingers are as cold as ice cubes.
>
> He ran as fast as a blink of an eye.
>
> Her voice sounded like someone was holding her nose.
>
> My mom cooks like a head chef at a four-star restaurant.

The words "as" and "like" clue you in to the presence of similes. Similes will help you to visualize information in your reading and further your understanding of the material.

40. Metaphors are like similes, but they do not use comparisons. Instead, a metaphor states that one thing is another thing to show a likeness. Here are some examples of metaphors:

> My classroom was an oven yesterday.
>
> She's a dolphin in the pool.
>
> Their house is a castle.

41. Idioms are common expressions that do not mean literally what the words say. Here are some examples:

Idiom	Meaning
Pull yourself together.	Regain your self-control.
I'll pull some strings and see what I can do for you.	I'll use my influence to help you.
Time to hit the hay.	Time to go to bed.
Hold your horses.	Don't rush ahead.
He always puts his foot in his mouth.	He always says something he should not.
She gets in everyone's hair.	She bothers everyone.

42. Make a list in your journal of similes, metaphors, and idioms you've come across. Study one or two a day until you've memorized all the meanings. Ask your family, friends, and teachers to contribute to your list. You may also ask a friend to quiz you once a week.

43. Figurative language is similar to idioms. These phrases cannot be interpreted literally. What they say is not what they mean, so you'll have to memorize the meanings of these phrases. Here are some examples:

Figurative Expressions	Meaning
He's as strong as an ox.	He is very strong.
It was raining cats and dogs.	It was raining heavily.
I've got a frog in my throat.	I'm having trouble talking clearly.
She has butterflies in her stomach.	She is nervous.

44. Write down some figurative expressions in your journal. Since figurative expressions have their own meanings, the more you know, the easier your understanding of them in your reading will be.

Chapter 5
Zooming Along: Tips for Increasing Your Speed

45. Increase your eye span. Try to read two or three words at a time instead of only one word. This will help you improve your reading comprehension because when you read words together, they make more sense than if you read one word at a time. Once you can read three words at a time, try reading four or five. Keep increasing you eye span by adding more words each time you read.

46. Try to read these two sentences. Which sentence do you read faster?

My / mother / told / me / to / go / to / the / store / and / buy / some / eggs, / milk, / and bread.

My mother / told me / to go / to the store / and buy / some eggs, / milk, / and bread.

47. Practice! If you read only one word at a time now, you will not be able to read two or three words at a time immediately. Practice reading larger and larger groups of words when reading for pleasure. Do not waste valuable study time learning how to increase your eye span. When you study, read at your normal pace to make sure you understand all the material.

48. One trick to help you increase your eye span is to focus on a space slightly above the word groups you are reading. This way, your vision will spread and you will be able to take in more words at one glance. If this does not work for you, try focusing on a space slightly to the left or right of the line you are reading. Can you read a larger group of words now?

49. Your return eye sweep is an important skill to improve upon as well. This is the movement your eyes make as they go from the end of one line to the beginning of the next. When you get to the end of a line, bring your eyes down and back to the beginning of the next line immediately. The faster the sweep, the faster your reading will be. Follow these examples.

When reading for speed, one should not read one word at a time. Instead, try to focus on two words with one glance. This will increase your reading speed as well as your comprehension.

This technique may seem difficult at first, but with a great deal of determination and practice you will be able to master this skill. Best of all, you will reap the benefits of faster reading and better comprehension for the rest of your life.

50. Recognizing word configurations can also help you increase your reading speed. Each word has its own special shape. Knowing the shape of familiar words means you can glance at them quickly and recognize them. Once you have mastered this skill, you will not need to focus on each word as you read.

51. Try to figure out what these words are by their shapes:

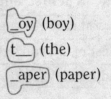

_oy (boy)

t_ (the)

_aper (paper)

Practice this exercise with a friend. Think of five words and draw their word shapes. Ask your friend to do the same. Exchange word shapes and figure out what the words are.

52. An author sometimes gives readers green lights to skip material. Phrases such as "for example" and "for instance" tell you if you already know the author's meaning, you do not need to spend time reading the example. This green light signals you to go ahead with your reading.

53. An author can also give readers yellow lights such as "however," "but," and "on the other hand." These words and phrases tell you to slow down because the author will be providing you with a contradictory thought. You will need to concentrate on what is coming next.

54. Vary your rate of reading speed for green light and yellow light signals to use your energy more efficiently and place your concentration where it belongs. The more you practice, the easier it will be to figure out when to speed up or slow down your reading speed.

55. Keep a sharp eye out for "negatives" in your reading. Often, when trying to read for speed, a reader may accidentally skip over "nots" and "don'ts" in sentences. This can change the whole meaning. For example:

John hadn't slept for three days.

John had slept for three days.

In the first sentence, John is exhausted. When the negative part of the sentence is omitted in the second sentence, however, John is very well rested.

56. Don't say the text aloud or to yourself as you read for pleasure. Although this technique can help increase your ability to memorize text and facts, it dramatically slows down your reading.

57. Don't use your finger, pen, or pencil to point at the words as you read. This extra step takes extra time and does not help increase comprehension. When you point to specific words your eye movements slow down, as does your reading rate.

58. It might not seem practical at first, but you can read with speed when studying. The first step is to *preread* the material. Read the title of the chapter, and all headings and subheadings within the chapter, to get a general overview of the material. Chapters are broken down into sections. Each section contains important concepts. By reading the headings and subheadings for each section you'll get a good introduction to the chapter. And it only takes a few minutes!

59. Look for words that are highlighted or in bold face. This special type is a signal to you that these concepts are important. Look at all graphs and pictures with captions. Many times an author will use a graph or picture to give the reader additional information about a specific idea.

60. Read the first and last sentences of every paragraph to get a better sense of the material. These sentences generally give a brief overview of all the information discussed in the paragraph.

61. Read the summary and the chapter questions before reading the chapter. You'll be able to pick out some of the key topics that will be covered in the chapter. You'll also know what answers to look for as you read.

62. Read each paragraph, then make notes of the main idea in each one. If you make your notes in question form, you can quiz yourself later with ease.

63. If you are looking for specific information, such as the date a particular event took place, do not read the entire chapter. Skim the material until you find what you're looking for. There's no point wasting time reading a lot of information you don't need to know right now. Go back and carefully read the chapter later.

64. When you come to the information you are looking for, read the sentence before it and after it to confirm that you are interpreting the information correctly.

65. When you read, try to anticipate what the author's conclusions will be. This will help you to focus on the material and remember more of what you've read.

66. Convert the first sentence of each paragraph into a question and look for the answer as you read the paragraph. This trick will increase your concentration and comprehension.

67. Use your own background and experiences to increase your comprehension of the material. When you read fiction, first evaluate each character's traits and actions according to the customs and values common to their time, place, and situation. Then compare the character's values to your own. Analyze each character's actions in relation to yourself and the society you live in.

68. Improve your speed and comprehension by performing daily drills. Time yourself for one page, five pages, and ten pages of reading. Record the times. Later in the week, time yourself again using the same book. Repeat every few days to continue building these skills. Try doing these drills with both fiction and nonfiction books. You can use the tips on page 75 to calculate the number of words you read per minute.

69. Speed reading can help you improve your test scores, too. Skim through an exam before you start answering questions. Often, answers to some questions are found in other questions. Scanning also helps you budget your time appropriately.

70. Don't waste time! Many speed readers wind up spending more time reading a text than they would if they read at normal speed by making these mistakes:

- **Problem:** Rereading entire portions of text because one part is difficult to understand.

  Solution: Use a pencil to underline the parts you will need to go back to later.

- **Problem:** Jumping ahead in the text, which means the reader must later go back.

  Solution: Skim through the text first to get an idea of what will be coming up.

Chapter 6
Ideas for Enhancing Your Comprehension Skills

71. Visit your neighborhood library and get acquainted with the materials in the collection. Most libraries have videos, stories on tape, games, magazines, and other nonbook materials in addition to thousands of books. Find out if any of these materials can help you improve your comprehension skills. Look through the subject card catalog under "Reading" to see what resources your library has.

72. Get a library card. It is your key to the world. Almost everything you will ever want or need to know is in a book. The more you read, the more knowledge you will have, the faster you will read, and the better your comprehension will be. The librarian will ask you to fill out a form. You may need to show proof of residence if your library is a public one. If you don't have something to show you live in town, your parent can show the librarian his/her driver's license.

73. Make friends with the librarians in your school and in your public library. They are an invaluable resource! Ask them for more tips to improve your reading and comprehension skills. Librarians are experts in helping you find whatever you need in the collection. They are there to help you—it's their job!

74. Familiarize yourself with all the different forms of writing—folktales, fables, legends, myths, romance, adventure, science fiction, drama, comedy, biographies, autobiographies, reference, nonfiction, fiction, newspapers, magazines, comic books. Spend some time each week reading one or two different writing forms. Remember to adjust your reading speed to the type of material you are reading.

75. Set a reading goal for each week. If you feel comfortable reading one book a week, do that. Write a brief summary of the book in your journal. This is a good way to test your comprehension skills. Then try to read a bit more the next week. Continue to build your reading goals until you are reading several books a week.

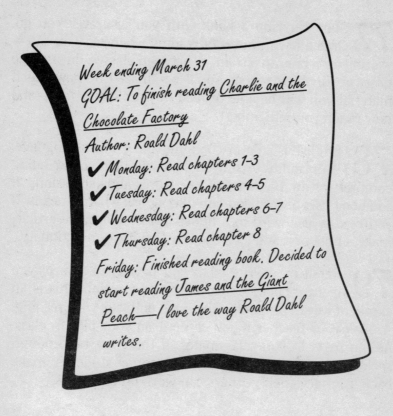

Week ending March 31
GOAL: To finish reading <u>Charlie and the Chocolate Factory</u>
Author: Roald Dahl
✔ Monday: Read chapters 1-3
✔ Tuesday: Read chapters 4-5
✔ Wednesday: Read chapters 6-7
✔ Thursday: Read chapter 8
Friday: Finished reading book. Decided to start reading <u>James and the Giant Peach</u>—I love the way Roald Dahl writes.

76. Try to vary your reading. If you only like to read mysteries, for example, go to the library and choose a nonfiction book about a mysterious subject. You'll probably be surprised at how many different types of books interest you.

77. Start carrying a book with you wherever you go. Grab a few minutes of reading whenever you can— waiting for a bus, on a train, in between classes, during free time, at lunch or recess. You'll be amazed by how much material you will be able to read in your spare time—and how much you remember!

78. English is an ever-changing and growing language. Your ability to stay current will help your reading comprehension. Be aware of new words and expressions. If someone uses a word you don't know, ask what it means. If you read a new word in a newspaper or magazine article, make a note of it and look the word up in your dictionary.

79. Retell or rewrite what you have read as a play, a picture book, a soap opera, or a script. This is an excellent way to remember the main points of your reading.

Ask your teacher if you can put on your play in class. Assign parts to your classmates. If there are not enough speaking parts for everyone, let some students make background scenery. Others can work on costumes.

80. Write an introduction, an epilogue, a different ending, or an additional chapter to a book you are reading. This will increase your understanding of the material. Share your insights with the class. You may think up a better ending to a story than the author did!

81. Read a nonfiction book and try to interpret its meaning in three different ways: literally, inferentially, and critically. Write your interpretations in your journal and ask your teacher to critique them.

82. Design a bookmark or jacket cover for one of your favorite books, or make a poster based on the main ideas. The cover should show one of the most exciting or important scenes from the book.

83. Keep a diary from the point of view of one of the characters. As you read, write down your thoughts about the character's personality, her feelings about other characters in the book, her goals and dreams. When you've finished the book, go back and read your diary. When you are tested on the book, you will be able to answer the questions more fully based on your observations. You may want to share your diary with your teacher.

84. Create a diorama, a mural, or a slide show. This is a great way to show others how well you understood the book. Ask your teacher if you can present your project to the class. Be prepared to answer questions about the book.

85. Create an advertisement for a book you have read and enjoyed. What would you tell your classmates about this book that would make them want to read it? Try to focus on an exciting moment in the story to hook your friends.

86. Make a comic strip based on the action of your book.

KIDNAPPED

by Robert Louis Stevenson

Do you love suspense, mystery, and heart-stopping excitement? Then read this exciting tale of deceit, courage, and friendship set in 18th-century Scotland. You'll be on the edge of your seat when young David Balfour is sold into slavery by his conniving uncle. You'll rejoice when Davy is rescued by Alan Breck. And you'll be thrilled when Davy takes revenge on his uncle.

**Don't wait—read
KIDNAPPED now!**

Chapter 7
Understanding Is the Key to Reading Success

87. Survey your class about one piece of information in a book you have all read and make a graph illustrating the results. Be sure to include each student's answer. You can make a bar graph, a pie graph, or a chart. Display the graph in the classroom and be prepared to answer questions. Make index cards outlining the key concepts in the text to prompt you in case you don't recall the answer.

88. Research information about the author. How did he or she get the idea for the book? Did the material come from any personal experiences in the author's life? Why did the author decide to become a writer? By getting to know the author you will have a better understanding of the book.

89. Read the copy on the back cover or jacket flap of a book. This text usually summarizes the essence of the book, and provides important clues about the main ideas of the text.

90. If reviews are cited on the back of the book, read them. Aside from offering the opinions of experts whose work is relevant to the book's topic, reviews can instantly put you in the right frame of mind. For example, what types of book would have received the following reviews?

"A rollercoaster ride of thrills and chills!"
—J. T. Smith

"One of the most thorough and intense studies of post-World War II Germany ever written."
—Alice Jackson

Don't be put off if a book has received poor reviews. Even though critics may not have liked the book you may still find it worthwhile. Be your own judge!

91. Check the copyright date of every book. Knowing when a book was published can help you better understand works of fiction. If you'd like more background information, you can research the time period to get a clear overview of the customs and lifestyles of the people. For nonfiction books, the date of publication is essential to knowing whether the information is current. If the copyright date in a textbook is a few years old, check with your librarian to see if a new edition of the book has been published. Textbooks are usually revised every four to five years to keep the information current.

92. The table of contents provides an excellent outline for a book. Read it carefully as preparation for reading the text. Jot down questions that come to mind as you read the table of contents, and look for the answers when you read the text.

93. Always read the foreword to a book. The foreword tells you about the author and the text that you are about to read. Many people skip over this part, wanting to get started with the actual book. But the information in the foreword can be invaluable in helping you understand why the author wrote the book and his/her reasons for choosing certain kinds of information.

94. If your reading material contains graphs, charts, photographs, or other visuals, take the time to carefully study them and their captions. Many of the main points of a book or article will be included in these illustrations.

95. Don't attempt to read statistical information quickly. Scan the headings of a chart or graph to identify the topic, then go back and read the text that explains the graph. When you have finished reading the accompanying text, return to the statistics to study them carefully. You may find it helpful to jot down some of the more important information on index cards to review later.

You may find that many of the important concepts discussed in the text are included in the chart or graph. If that is true, study the graph and note how the information has been organized. Then try to memorize the chart or graph. When you begin to prepare for a test on this material, recreate the graph and ask yourself what the information means. You can review a great deal of information in a short time.

96. When you're done reading a book—you're not really done! If the book has an index, be sure to read it as a way to check your memory and comprehension. If terms in the index are unclear, go back to those sections in the book and refresh your memory. If you continue to have trouble with some concepts, make index cards for them. You can also ask your teacher or a friend to explain any concepts you have difficulty remembering.

97. The glossary, which provides definitions of important concepts discussed in a book, is another constructive way to test your knowledge of the material you have read. If you can skim through a glossary and readily identify all the words it contains, chances are you have a good grasp of the material and will do well on a test.

98. Remember to take short breaks from reading and studying. A tired reader is not an efficient reader! Get up and exercise, get a snack, or call a friend. These small rewards give your brain some time to absorb information and help keep you fresh. But don't take too many breaks!

99. In your journal, write down your reactions, new vocabulary, and anything that comes to mind while reading. Review your journal frequently to keep new ideas fresh in your memory. Ask a friend to swap journals with you. Each person has unique thoughts and ideas. You can learn a lot from your friend's observations.

100. Remember that reading is supposed to be fun. If you're not enjoying yourself, read something else that appeals to you more. If you're doing reading for school that can't be avoided, plan to reward yourself for completing an assignment. If you know that you will be able to do something fun once the assignment is finished, you will be more motivated.

101. Give yourself a pat on the back for improving your reading skills. Remember that a great reader can master any new challenge that comes along! Also remember that good reading skills will be an asset as you continue your school career and beyond. Continue to improve your reading skills throughout your life.

APPENDIX

Calculate Your Reading Rate

Some of the most effective methods for increasing your reading speed have been discussed in this book. But did you know there is also a way to measure exactly how much your reading rate has improved?

First you have to figure out what your **initial reading rate** is. This is the number of words you read in one minute right now. To calculate your initial reading rate, you will need a timer or a watch with a second hand. If you use a watch you may want to ask a friend or a parent to help with this.

---

1. Sit in a comfortable chair with a book opened to a page of text. Ideally, there should not be any illustrations, charts, or graphs on the page. You can use a textbook or a novel.

2. Set the timer for one minute and begin reading. If you are using a watch, start reading when the timekeeper says, "Go."

3. Read at your regular speed. When the timer goes off, stop reading. If you are using a watch, stop reading when the timekeeper says, "Stop."

---

4. Count the number of words in five full lines (not sentences). Count only the words—do not count any punctuation marks.

5. Round off the total number of words to the nearest number divisible by five. Divide this number by five. This number is the average number of words per line in the passage you've just read.

6. Count the number of lines on a typical page. Do not count the lines of the first page of a chapter, because there are usually fewer lines on these pages.

7. Multiply the number of words per line (from step #5) by the number of lines per page. Your answer tells you the average number of words on each text page.

8. Go back and count how many pages of text you read in one minute. Multiply that number by the average number of words on a text page (from step #7). This number tells you how many words you read per minute right now.

To improve your reading rate, go though this book and practice the tips for increasing reading speed. Give yourself enough time to master one technique before moving on to another. When you have successfully mastered several of the techniques, try the above exercise again. Your reading rate should have increased. Keep practicing, and you'll see dramatic improvements in your reading speed.

The "I" Hand Motion

If you are reading a narrow column of text, such as a newspaper article, the "I" Hand motion is a great way to increase your reading speed. The technique is simple but remember—this only works on narrow columns of text.

1. Sit in a comfortable chair at a table. Spread a newspaper in front of you and choose an article to read.

2. Place your hand at the top of the article (you choose whichever hand is more comfortable). Move your hand from left to right over the first two lines of the column.

3. Move your hand down the center of the column. Stop at the line above the last two lines in the column.

4. Move your hand from left to right across the last two lines of the column.

Many times the first two lines of an article contain a brief explanation of what the article is about. Tha last two lines will often sum up the key points of the article. This technique is effective for a quick read of the paper to familiarize yourself with what is going on in the world. If you want more in-depth knowledge about a certain topic, read the article carefully.

Here are some examples of how the "I" Hand Motion works:

Although it takes
a lot of time and
practice to become
a better reader, you
will develop a lifelong
love of reading and
feel good about all
that you have accomplished.

There are many
different techniques
you can use to
increase your reading
speed, but none of
them will be effective
unless you understand
the material.

 **Recommended Reading**

These books have one thing in common: kids love them!

Among the Dolls by William Sleator, Dutton, 1975. A girl gets a dollhouse for her birthday, then gets drawn inside it and tormented by the dolls she mistreated the day before.

Call It Courage by Armstrong Sperry, Macmillan, 1971. A boy who lives on a South Sea island and is afraid of the sea overcomes his fears.

The Iron Giant: A Story in Five Nights by Ted Hughes, Harper, 1987. A giant who roams the land unchallenged is confronted by an alien and must fight for his life.

Caddie Woodlawn by Carol Ryrie Brink, Macmillan, 1973. The story of a pioneer girl who has run-ins with Native Americans, plays pranks, and gets into schoolhouse fights.

On My Honor by Marion Dane Bauer, Dell, 1987. A boy goes swimming with his friend, who drowns. He returns home denying the incident happened.

From the Mixed-Up Files of Mrs. Basil E. Frankweiler by E. L. Konigsburg, Dell, 1986. A girl and her brother run away to the Metropolitan Museum of Art.

The Indian in the Cupboard by Lynne Reid Banks, Avon, 1983. A boy's toy Indian comes to life and he must care for him.

James and the Giant Peach by Roald Dahl, Puffin, 1988. A boy who lives with his mean aunts discovers a magical peach in the backyard and the characters who inhabit it.

Dinky Hocker Shoots Smack by M. E. Kerr, Dell, 1972. Dinky Hocker has, among other problems, an addiction to food. The story tells of her feelings for her own problems as well as those of her mother and brother.

The Day They Came to Arrest the Book by Nat Hentoff, Delacorte, 1982. *The Adventures of Huckleberry Finn* becomes the focus of a group of students and parents who want the book banned from the school because of its racist and sexist views.

The Outsiders by S. E. Hinton, G. K. Hall & Co., 1967. This story focuses on Ponyboy, his brothers Sodapop and Darry, and their circle of friends. They find themselves trying to understand parents who are far from perfect, living on the wrong side of town, having little money, and dealing with the "socs," the in-crowd of kids in town.

The Divorce Express by Paula Danziger, Delacorte,

1982. In this story, Phoebe lives with her father in Woodstock, New York, during the week and with her mother in Manhattan on the weekends. She takes a bus back and forth between the two places and meets Rosie, another teen whose parents have divorced and live far apart.

The Secret of Sarah Revere by Ann Rinaldi, Gulliver Books, 1995. When Sarah's father, Paul Revere, goes off on one of his missions, family friend Dr. Joseph Warren comes to watch over the family. But Sarah feels he is too attentive to her mother. As if that were not enough, war breaks out and Sarah must somehow cope with all that happens.

The Curse of the Blue Figurine by John Bellairs, Bantam, 1984. A boy steals an ancient book from a church and evil things begin happening.

The Hobbit by J. R. R. Tolkien, Houghton Mifflin, 1938. Bilbo Baggins, your average stay-at-home hobbit, is tricked into going on a quest to faraway lands where he encounters dwarfs, goblins, elves, trolls, magic, and evil beyond anything he could have imagined.

The Lion, the Witch, and the Wardrobe by C. S. Lewis, Macmillan, 1988. Four children find the entrance to a magical land called Narnia thorough the back of a wardrobe. They find themselves in the middle of a struggle between the creatures who inhabit the place and the White Witch, who wishes to control all of Narnia.

Ghosts I Have Been by Richard Peck, Dell, 1977. After a girl's mother reads her fortune from tea leaves, things begin happening. The girl finds herself on an ill-fated ship, the *Titanic,* where she meets the ghost of a boy who died on the ocean liner's maiden voyage.

Then Again, Maybe I Won't by Judy Blume, Macmillan, 1971. Tony and his family have just moved to Long Island, New York, and he must adjust to the many changes he finds in his new surroundings.

Bibliography

Berg, Howard Stephen. *Super Reading Secrets*. New York, NY: Warner Books, Inc., 1992.

Board of Education of the City of New York. *Essential Learning Outcomes: Communication Arts*. New York, NY: Board of Education of the City of New York, 1988.

Coman, Marcia J., and Kathy L. Heavers. *What You Need to Know About Reading Comprehension & Speed, Skimming and Scanning, Reading for Pleasure*. (NTC Skill Builders series), Lincolnwood, IL: National Textbook Company, 1995.

Heilman, Arthur W., Timothy Blair, and William Rupley. *Principles and Practices of Teaching Reading*. Columbus, OH: Charles E. Merrill, 1994.

The Reading Laboratory. *Double Your Reading Speed*. New York, NY: Ballantine Books, 1985.

Routman, Regie. *Invitations: Changing as Teachers and Learners, K-12*. Portsmouth, NH: Heinemann, 1991.

Terban, Marvin. *In a Pickle & Other Funny Idioms*. New York, NY: Clarion Books, 1983.

———*It Figures: Fun Figures of Speech*. New York, NY: Clarion Books, 1993.

———*Punching the Clock: Funny Action Idioms*. New York, NY: Clarion Books, 1990.

———*Your Foot's on My Feet! and Other Tricky Nouns*. New York, NY: Clarion Books, 1986.

Zorn, Robert. *Speed Reading*. New York, NY: HarperPerennial, 1991.

Answers

page 16
    a—literal; b—critical; c—inferential

pages 25–29
descriptive; collection; cause-and-effect; response; comparison

Index

Look for all the books in the

101 Ways

series

101 Ways to Do Better in School
0-8167-3285-X $2.95 U.S. / $4.25 CAN.

101 Ways to Get Straight A's
0-8167-3565-4 $2.95 U.S. / $4.25 CAN.

101 Ways to Boost Your Writing Skills
0-8167-3835-1 $2.95 U.S. / $4.25 CAN.

101 Ways to Boost Your Math Skills
0-8167-3836-X $2.95 U.S. / $4.25 CAN.

101 Ways to Take Tests With Success
0-8167-4225-1 $2.95 U.S. / $4.25 CAN.

101 Ways to Read With Speed and Understanding
0-8167-4226-X $2.95 U.S. / $4.25 CAN.

Available wherever you buy books.

Troll

Do you have a minute?

Then take the *One-Minute Challenge*. These books are packed with tricky challenges to test your basic skills in math, English, and vocabulary. With answers in the back of each book, these quizzes are a perfect primer for the SAT's. Earn better grades starting today!

Notes

Notes